The Ancient Franciscan Friary Of Bun-Na-Margie, Ballycastle, On The North Coast Of Antrim

Francis Joseph Bigger

In the interest of creating a more extensive selection of rare historical book reprints, we have chosen to reproduce this title even though it may possibly have occasional imperfections such as missing and blurred pages, missing text, poor pictures, markings, dark backgrounds and other reproduction issues beyond our control. Because this work is culturally important, we have made it available as a part of our commitment to protecting, preserving and promoting the world's literature. Thank you for your understanding.

THE ANCIENT FRANCISCAN
Friary of Bun-na-Margie,
BALLYCASTLE,
ON THE NORTH COAST OF ANTRIM:

BEING A DESCRIPTIVE AND HISTORICAL NOTICE OF THIS
ONCE CELEBRATED FRIARY, SO INTIMATELY ASSOCIATED
WITH THE FAMILY OF MACDONNELL, EARLS OF ANTRIM.

BY

FRANCIS JOSEPH BIGGER,

*Member of the Royal Irish Academy; Fellow of the Royal Society of Antiquaries;
Honorary Secretary of the Belfast Naturalists' Field Club;
Editor of the Ulster Journal of Archæology.*

WITH PLANS AND DRAWINGS BY WILLIAM J. FENNELL,
ARCHITECT, BELFAST.

Belfast:
MARCUS WARD & CO., LIMITED,
ROYAL ULSTER WORKS;
LONDON, SYDNEY, AND NEW YORK.

THE FRIARY OF BUN-NA-MARGIE,
CO. ANTRIM.

TO MY VENERABLE AND ESTEEMED FRIEND,

THE REV. GEORGE HILL,

I DEDICATE THESE PAGES,

AS A SLIGHT TOKEN OF THANKS
FOR THE HELPING HAND SO FREELY EXTENDED TO ME,
AND THE WISE COUNSEL GIVEN
IN ALL MATTERS
RELATING TO OUR LOCAL HISTORY.

F. J. B.

ARDRIE, BELFAST,
March, 1898.

REFERENCES.

IN the following pages I have not cumbered the text with authorities, as books of reference to my subject are few and much used, but I must freely acknowledge the sources of my information. In the forefront stands *The MacDonnells of Antrim*, by the Rev. George Hill—a vast storehouse of knowledge, local and far-reaching—than which no book was ever more carefully and accurately penned by historian, without taint of partizanship, fear, or prejudice. I am also indebted to that great work, *The Ecclesiastical Antiquities of Down and Connor and Dromore*, by the late Bishop Reeves; and also *The Diocese of Down and Connor*, by the Rev. James O'Laverty—three works by three Ecclesiastics of different shades of thought and belief of whom any Diocese might well feel proud.

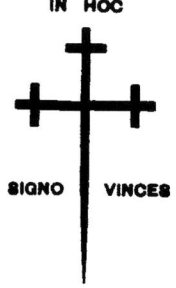

MacDonnell.   MacQuillin.

The Friary of Bun-na-margie,

in the Parish Culfeightrin, Barony of Carey, and Glynns of Antrim.

The Cross over the Grave of Julia MacQuillin.

Bun-na-margie has few annals of the past, and its architectural remains are but scant and unimportant when compared with the other great religious houses of the Middle Ages. Nevertheless, its associations are of deep interest, not only to the casual tourist, but to the surrounding people, whose ancestors mingled in the incidents connected with its history, and now lie buried beneath the shadow of its crumbling walls.

General Remarks.

The site of the Monastery is in itself one of great beauty and attractiveness, and must have afforded constant delight and satisfaction to the habited occupiers when the Friary was in its early glory, as it does still to all who visit its roofless nave and gaze upon its great shattered window.

We can readily picture the friars, on a bright Easter morning, trooping out of the beautiful western door of their church after the early service, with the resounding *Te Deum* and the music of the songs of exultation still ringing in their ears, to gaze up at the great dome of Knoc-lade clearly cutting into the blue sky, the fleecy clouds chasing each other like lambs across the valley of Glenshesk, with the winding waters of the Margie dancing over their pebbly bed in the sunlight close at hand, the deep pools sheltered by the hazel woods, or the overhanging banks affording ample shelter for the speckled trout which largely supplied the table of these Franciscan brothers.

To the north and the east stretched the long piled-up sand-dunes, against which the great waves of the Atlantic dashed and thundered in the winter's wind, unchecked by the far-away breakwater of the rugged island of Raghery, or gently broke in white foam along the pebbly beach in the setting sun of a summer's day.

To the right, Benmore rises from the sea, at first with a stair-like slope, then upright as a pine cleaving the sky, tremendous and ever beautiful, whether in sunshine or shade, calm or storm, its massive

DUN-RAINEY, BUN-NA-MARGIE, AND CARRIG-USNACH, BALLYCASTLE, CO. ANTRIM.
From a drawing by John Vinycomb.

brow ever speaking of power and majesty. Nearer at hand, sheltered by the white crescent of Kenbann, nestled the port of MacDonnell's Castle, long known as Margie-town. Here, by the pure stream, Religion has left her mark by the hand of the monk.

Such were the surroundings of the Friary of Bun-na-margie, and such they still remain, affording prospects not to be surpassed on our northern coast. But it cannot be said that the advantages of the locality called forth the house. The district around Ballycastle has a history reaching to the earliest eras, deep into the misty past of the mythical age long anterior to Christianity. Had not the children of Usnach landed in the bay on their fateful return from Glen Etive, and are not their wanderings and the love they bore each other still told in the Antrim glens? When the first stone of the Friary was laid, the ramparts of Dun-Rainey, within an arrow-shot, bore evidences of a

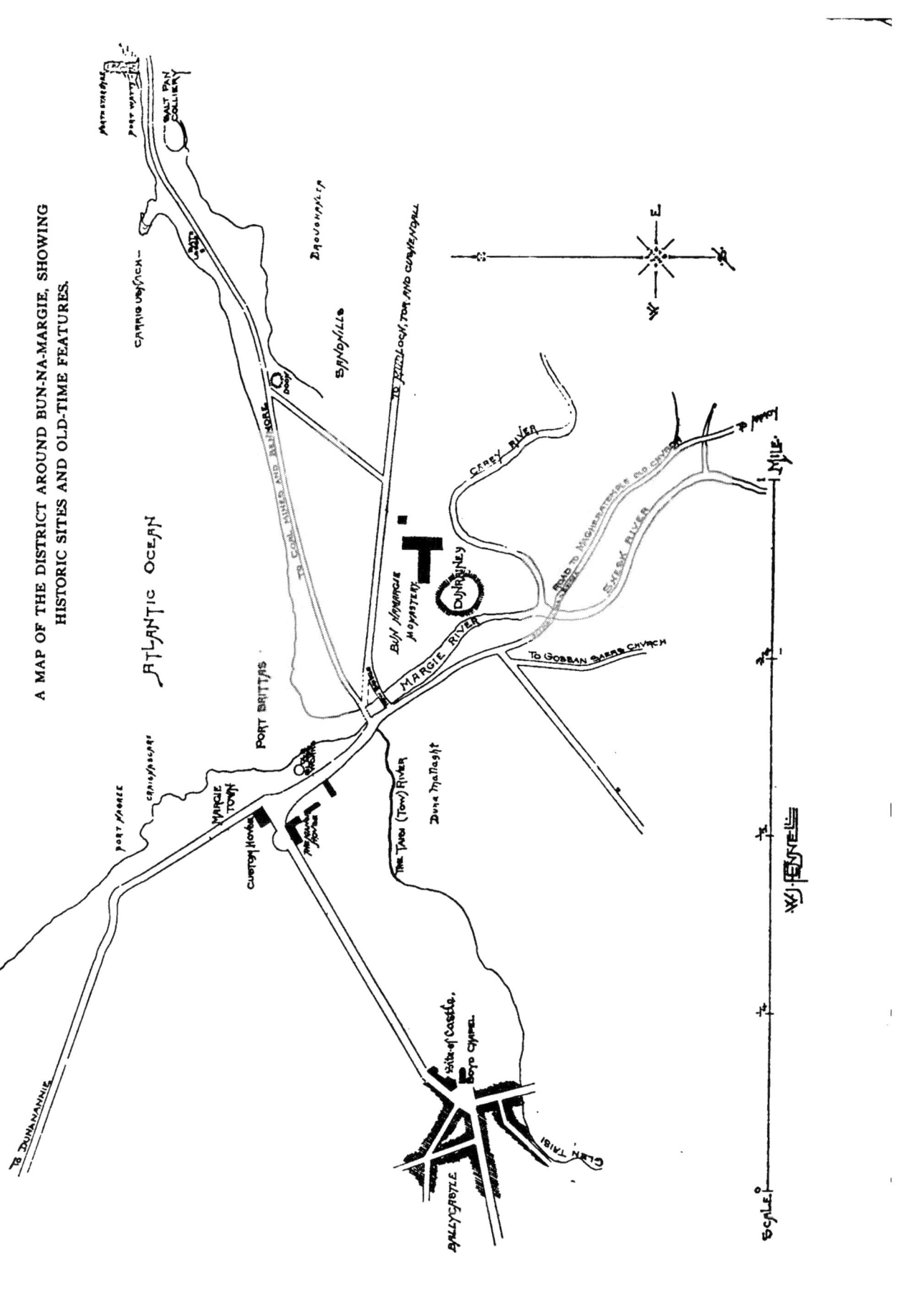

regal habitation, whilst the great carn on Knoc-lade spoke of a Royal grave reddened by the rays of the rising sun and gilded with its setting glory.

The immediate cause of the sacred edifice rearing its many gables on the river's bank is unknown, but doubtless it was founded by some princely clan; for the mediæval chieftain, whilst fully relying upon the strength of his own right arm, depended also upon the prayers of the religious during life, and more especially the care bestowed upon the dead, when each warrior was laid to rest in his coat of armour, his sword by his side, within the precincts of the choir,—or some fair maid was snatched away in the bloom of youth from the castle's bower, or aged mother who perhaps had seen her many sons borne to their tombs before she had been laid beside her departed lord. Thus it was that every princely house founded at least one Monastery, where the rites of religion could be administered with befitting pomp and pageantry, within whose church all the clan could crowd to see the nuptial ceremony, or assemble at the great thanksgiving, when the chief, safely returned from strife laden with the spoils of victory, never forgetting a due and proper offering for the house, implored rest for the souls of his ancestors and those fallen in battle; or, as was often the case, the piercing *cabine* of the mourners was heard, as the corpse of the warrior was borne shoulder high by his clansmen and followers along the strand to the abbey's gate, there to be met and received—mangled and pierced as it was—by the men of peace, and borne down the darkened aisle to dirge and funeral chant, amidst the wailing of followers and the muttered vows of revenge.

> "Lay their spears and bucklers bright
> By the warriors' sides aright;
> Lay upon the low grave floor,
> 'Neath each head, the blue claymore;
> Lay the collars, as is meet,
> Of their greyhounds at their feet;
> In the falcon's jesses throw,
> Hook and arrow, line and bow."
>
> *Sir S. Ferguson.*

All the glamour of these old-time customs have passed away with the extinguished glories of Bun-na-margie, and the bare walls, once resonant with prayers and psalms, now only re-echo the plaintive notes of the sea-birds as they poise themselves aloft above its deserted cloisters, or the swish of the mower's scythe is heard in the rich meadows where the dead lie thick together, or the cry of the landrail resounds through the vaults in the hush of a warm June night. To the antiquary alone remains the duty, in these later days, to gather up the fragments of the past and piece them together, so that some image, with many cracks and many defects it may be, can be seen and recorded for the present and future ages.

It is said that the Franciscans founded their first house in Ireland at Youghal about 1224, just at the time when the enthusiasm kindled by the Crusades was at its height throughout England and the Continent, and when all the religious orders flourished at their best. The followers of Saint Francis of Assisi were noted for their vows of poverty and charity, and many remarkable legends are recorded of the early members of the Order. As to the exact date of the foundation of the Friary we can find no record. By some it is stated that it was founded as early as A.D. 1202 by William de Burgo " To the Honour of God and the Virgin ;" and some credence is given to this by the early seventeenth century inscription on the Antrim vault, "*In dei deimatrisque virginis honorem.*" Whether this is merely the coincidence of the use of a favourite dedication or not we cannot say, but it is recorded in the *Monasticon Hibernicum* that "about the year 1202 William de Burgh granted the Village of Ardimur, with the Church and all its appurtenances, to Richard, one of the monks of Glastonbury, to found a priory to the honour of God and the Virgin Mary." At this period William de Burgo was Earl of Ulster, and nominally had these lands in his possession ; and if he was the first of the sept MacQuillin—which, however, is disputed—it would certainly go to explain why this clan always claimed Bun-na-margie as a foundation of their family. The De Burgos were Lords of Connacht, and became entitled to the Earldom of Ulster, now vested in the British Sovereign, by marriage with De Lacy's daughter. It is told that Richard de Burgo, the red earl, brought the MacQuillins from Connacht and the Bissetts from Scotland to keep the O'Neills in check. In later years the MacDonnells claimed these lands by descent from the Bissetts and by conquest from the MacQuillins, whilst the O'Neills never missed an opportunity of harrying the MacDonnells and disputing their claim. In a manuscript list, in the British Museum, of Franciscan monasteries in Ireland, it is recorded that Bun-na-margie was founded by Roy MacQuillin in the year 1500 ; thus again, although at a different date, its foundation is ascribed to a MacQuillin. No reliable authority has ever given the erection of this Monastery to the MacDonnells, although, as the conquerors and successors of the

Foundation.

MacQuillins, they assumed its patronage and made it their burial-place, and with their name it is now chiefly associated.

The general architecture of the ruins bears out its early foundation, probably the 14th century, although here and there later features are to be observed; but before we treat of them more fully, we desire to exhaust as far as possible the historic references to our subject. Of course the fateful year, 1537, saw the suppression of this Monastery with all the others throughout the kingdom; but being situated in a remote district, with the lord and the people still favourable to the Monastery, it is not to be supposed that *suppression* meant an immediate expulsion of the monks from its walls, for it is known that they lingered about its aisles for many years afterwards, nor did they finally leave until the MacDonnells had embraced the

Suppression.

BUN-NA-MARGIE—EAST WALL—EXTERIOR VIEW.

reformed faith, although during that time their existence had been checkered and filled with much adversity, and their numbers had dwindled to insignificance.

Bishop Magennis's confirmation.

The last great religious ceremony associated with the name of Bun-na-margie is that recorded in the *Spicelégium Ossoriense*, when Dr. Bonaventure Magennis, a Franciscan, confirmed about 700 Highland Scots in the month of October, 1639. The Scottish islanders were refugees from the bitter Covenanting persecutions which were commenced in that year against the Roman Catholics in particular. Amongst them was the Laird of Largie (a MacDonnell), who died at Bun-na-margie and was buried there. So endeared were the old walls to the Scots, that they long continued to flock in great numbers every year to Ballycastle, during the fair, to visit their kinsmen and to form alliances of a more lasting nature. It must have been a pathetic scene this confirmation of the Highlanders—the big rugged men, with their Gaelic tongue, barbaric costume, and fierce

THE FRIARY OF BUN-NA-MARGIE.

weapons, prostrate before the bishop of their old faith, receiving a rite that their country had discarded, amidst surroundings that their nation had decreed idolatrous and profane.

Bishop Magennis sojourned with his relative, Randall, first Earl of Antrim, who had before this got into trouble for harbouring "Romish priests." In 1621, he had been summoned to Dublin by the Lord Deputy, Grandison, to answer such a charge, and Lord Antrim appealed to the King, pleading guilty, and receiving the King's pardon, "in respect that he has so ingeniously acknowledged his errors, and faithfully promised not to fall into the like again."

Bun-na-margie must then have been repaired, for around its walls, *Burning of the Friary.* from the year 1559, the renowned Sorley Boy MacDonnell had fought the MacQuillins many times with fatal results to them; but the great disaster to the Friary occurred in this wise. In January, 1584, the English, under Sir John Perrott, were pressing the Scots very hard on the North coast; they had taken Dunluce, and were now at Ballycastle. Sir Henry Wallop was cursing his fate in having to land stores from the ships on rafts in Margietown Bay. Captain Carlisle and Captain Warren had their men and horses lodged in the Church of Bun-na-margie, with two companies encamped close by, when "about 11 of the clok the same nyght came certayne troupes of Skottes on foote, and aboute vi horsemen with them, who had upon their staves wadds lyghted, wherewyth they sodaynly sett the roofe of the churche, being thatched, on fyer. They gave us a brave camisado, and entered our campe. The alarme being geven, I came forth in my shert, and at our first encounter, my men answeringe with mee verrie gallantlie, we put them off the ground, where the left one of their men that was emongst them of greate accompte; he was Sorlles gydon. They would fayne have had him away, but they were so plyed with Shotte that they left him and the field also, and fell to ronnynge away; where our horsemen might have done good servis, they were so pestered in the church that they coulde not get forthe theire horses in time to doo anythinge, and yet the skermish contynued three quarters of an owre. Ther wer bornt in the church seven horses and hackneys. I had slayne my sergeant and one armed man, William Jones. Captain Carleille had one killed and eight hurte, and I had twelve choys men hurte and myself with arrows in the raynes of my bak as I called forward my men in the arme and in the flanke and through the thigh, of which wounds I am verie sore, although I trust in God I shall recover it."

Sir John Perrott, Lord Deputy of Ireland, writing in the same year

1584, to Sir Francis Walsingham, the English Secretary of State, says: "For a token I have sent you Holy Columkill's crosse—a god of great veneration with Surley Boy and all Ulster; for so great was his grace, as happy he thought himself that coulde gett a kisse of the said crosse. I send him unto you that when you have made some sacrifice to him according to the disposition you beare to idolatrie, you maie, if you please, bestowe him upon my good Lady Walsingham or my Lady Sidney to weare as a Jewell of weight and bignesse, and not of prise and goodness, upon some solempne feaste or triumph daie at the Courte." The Lord Deputy had just gone to Ulster against Sorley Boy, and Saint Columbcille's Cross was part of the spoil he had carried away. This valuable relic was long preserved on Tory Island, but how it came into possession of the MacDonnells is unrecorded. The date of this letter corresponds with the time the English held Bun-na-margie; the relics and valuables of the house must have fallen into their hands, and this would explain how the Cross came into the possession of Perrott to be bestowed "upon my good Lady Walsingham." If it had been in the private possession of Sorley Boy, or even in his castle, it would have been carefully preserved; but the capture of the Monastery was unexpected, and so the Cross came as a spoil to the English. Its existence is now uncertain: perhaps it may still be preserved unknown, in a cabinet of some ducal house; or, alas! its jewels may have been taken from its case to form a newer fashion in ladies' trinkets, and the remainder cast aside as worthless.

In the despatch of Captain Warren more detail concerning the injury to the men is given than the damage done to the Monastery. The incident, however, dates the destruction of the church, and doubtless the domestic buildings also, for the fire must have been great when the horses were destroyed that had been stabled within its walls. The confirmation of the Highlanders took place in Bun-na-margie, which had then been repaired and the beautiful east window added, and not at the *locus refugii* of the monks in Ardagh at the top of Glenshesk, where they afterwards lingered when the Friary had been taken from them and their religion proscribed. Here they found a temporary home, with others of their Order, when the roofs had disappeared from the walls they loved so dearly, and their most sacred spots desecrated, their altars cast down, and the graves and monuments of the illustrious dead levelled with the ground. With what sad eyes and lingering looks they must have beheld their venerated house, as they hurried to and fro from their secret haunt in the vale of Glenshesk to the little harbour at Margietown, as they took ship to the securer isles of the Western Hebrides, or sailed away to the sunny land of France, to the vine-clad houses of their brethren by the banks of the Rhone and the Loire. Times had changed, and no more for them was Bun-na-margie to be a mother. The deep-sounding breakers on the neighbouring strand were to make midnight music for other ears, and the high-dashing spray on Carrig-Usnach was to be seen by other eyes; whilst the lark of the meadow was to sing matins over crumbling walls, and the plaintive notes of the curlew were alone to sound the funeral dirge of those whose souls had crossed the bar.

The community was of the Third Order of Franciscans, but by the decree of the Director-General, dated 15th August, 1687, Bun-na-margie became a Monastery of Franciscans *Strictioris Observantiæ*. This was when the few remaining members of the order had gone into their *locus refugii* in Glenshesk, having joined some Carrickfergus brethren of the latter order. Guardians were appointed until 1837, but such appointments were only nominal, as any community had long ceased to exist.

Sorley Boy MacDonnell, the youngest son of Alexander MacDonnell, was head of the clan during the latter part of the sixteenth century; but we need not here dwell upon his daring and prowess, save to point out what manner of man he was. He lived to see at least four of his brothers laid to rest in Bun-na-margie. His wife, Mary O'Neill, daughter of Con, first Earl of Tyrone, was buried with her own people at Armagh. By the way, a curious story is told of a monk travelling from the primatial city to Glenarm to beg the body of Shane O'Neill, who had been slain by the MacDonnells. "Father," said he, addressing a friar, "I come from our brothers of Armagh to beg the body of Shane O'Neill, so that we may bury it beside his ancestors in Armagh." The friar replied, "Have you," said he, "brought with you the remains of James MacDonnell, Lord of Antrim and Cantire, who was buried amongst the strangers of Armagh?" The answer was that he had not done so. "Then," replied the friar, "whilst you continue to tread on James, Lord of Antrim and Cantire, know ye that we here in Glenarm will continue to tread on the dust of your great O'Neill."

<small>Sorley Boy MacDonnell.</small>

This same Shane the Proud had, at the dictates of Queen Elizabeth, but doubtless also to serve his own ambition, defeated the MacDonnells with tremendous slaughter in Glentaise, not far from the walls of Bun-na-margie, and had taken Sorley Boy a prisoner, releasing him two years later at Cushendun, when he sought help from the clan he had so fearfully harried such a short time before. Sorley Boy had driven

<small>Shane O'Neill.</small>

the English from Carrickfergus—had fought the Queen's forces at Newry—had burned in his castle-yard of Dunanannie on the point of his sword the grant of his lands which Queen Elizabeth had bestowed upon him, saying what he had won by the sword he did not intend to hold by parchment. The year 1590 saw this turbulent chieftain, this the greatest of all the MacDonnells, laid beside the bones of his kindred in the old Friary of his ancestors; but now there are

Death of Sorley Boy.

> "No sigh to regret thee,
>   No eye to rain o'er thee,
>   No dirge to lament thee,
>   No friend to deplore thee!"
>
>   *J. J. Collanan.*

In contrast to his particularly wild and stormy career, Sorley died in bed in his castle of Dunanannie, overlooking the Bay of Ballycastle and the Franciscan Friary. "The faithful clansmen carried the remains of their brave old chieftain down the slope of the castle-hill, past the harbour where he had so often welcomed his Clandonnell kinsmen to the Antrim shore, and across the ford of the Margie, where the Irish *cabine* and the Highland *coronach* mingled in one wild wail for the dead." We can picture such a scene as this, the long wailing crowd descending the castle-crowned cliff with the coffin borne along by stalwart clansmen, and the old Friary with tolling bell sadly awaiting the approaching funeral train. Most of Sorley's children predeceased him, some falling by murder and treachery. In 1575 the Earl of Essex, finding out that the women and children of the MacDonnells had been sent to the island of Raghery for safety, despatched ships under Norris, who burned and slaughtered all upon the island. The proud English earl thought this a fair return for the defeats inflicted upon him in the open field. The chieftains were laid to rest within the walls of the church, the clansmen in the surrounding graveyard. A few years later saw this burial-ground for many seasons as red as a tilled hillside, with no grass growing there, so numerous were the burials; and even within recent memory a great pile of bones, collected from the adjoining fields, were heaped against the graveyard wall. They have since, however, received interment.

The slaughter on Raghery.

Sir Randal MacDonnell succeeded his father Sorley Boy, and his brother Angus, called Ultagh MacSorley, or the son of Sorley of Ulster, to distinguish him from his cousin Angus of Isla, disputed his possessions with him. Angus was an officer in the Earl of Tyrone's army, and survived the disastrous overthrow which Tyrone sustained

Sir Randal MacDonnell.

at Kinsale. In the dispute with his brother he was warmly supported by some of his kinsmen who opposed the proposed Royal grant from King James to Sir Randal. On one occasion, it is said, the two brothers met face to face, and blood would certainly have been spilled, the feud ran so high, had not a friar of Bun-na-margie, one O'Dornan, stood forth and rung a bell denouncing the curse of Saint Patrick against the wrongful claimant; whereupon Angus desisted from further contesting his brother's rights, which, later in the same year, 1603, were confirmed to him by the king "for the preservation of his own from the violence of his bad kinsmen."

The friar's curse.

A rude old perforated cross stands at the west end of the church, where the beautiful door formerly stood, and it is said to mark the grave of Julia MacQuillin, the "black nun" of Bun-na-margie. At her special request, which was no doubt prompted by her humility, she was buried at the doorway, so that all who entered the sacred building should tread upon her grave. She also requested that the coffin which might be used to carry her body to the grave should not be interred, but given to the next poor person who died, and that she be buried without a coffin. It is generally believed that Julia MacQuillin was a member of the family who had long ruled in these parts, and that she inherited all the pride and extravagance of her race. In later years, as a recluse, she sought the retirement of the Friary ruins, the date of her residence being about 1650. The little gate-house is still known by her name, and it may then have been sufficiently roofed to have afforded her the shelter she sought. She seems to have been more feared than liked, and wonderful prophecies made by her are still recorded. One weird but beautiful legend is worthy of repetition. On a wild stormy night the sinful sister of the "black nun" crept to the door of the cell where she was praying. The poor repentant woman implored her sister Julia to pray for her, but she would not answer, and upon being touched fled from the cell out into the graveyard, where she continued to pray in the storm. After a time she beheld issuing from the cell she had vacated beautiful gleams of light. Wondering at the sight she approached the cell, and, looking in, beheld her repentant sister kneeling on the floor with her hands in prayer in the centre of the gleam of light, and she heard a voice saying, "Come unto Me and I will give you rest," and her sister replied, "I come," and died, the light fading away. The "black nun" at once perceived how wicked she had been, and how her sinful sister was nearer heaven than she was, practising her austerities alone.

Julia MacQuillin.

After that night it is said she never ceased succouring the sick, the poor, and the fallen. Of poor Julia it may well be said—

> "Lay me in my hollow bed,
>   Grow the shamrocks over me;
>   Three in one and one in three,
>   Faith and hope and charity.
>   Peace and rest and silence be
> With me where you lay my head;
>   O dear the shamrocks are to me!"
>
> *Rosa Mulholland.*

Julia MacQuillin was a friend and visitor of Alice MacDonnell, first Countess of Antrim, who erected the great east window in the Friary about the time her husband erected the family vault (1621). The Countess was the daughter of Hugh O'Neill, the renowned Earl of Tyrone, and long survived her husband. After his death she left Dunluce and came to reside at Ballycastle, from whence she was

BUN-NA-MARGIE—EAST SECTION—INTERIOR VIEW, SHOWING REFECTORY, CHAMBER, PASSAGE, CHURCH, VAULT.

driven to take shelter amongst her own people in the valleys of Tyrone by the hordes of covenanted Scots who came over in 1642 to take part in the wars of that period. Not until the Restoration was the widowed Countess permitted to enjoy her dowry lands at Ballycastle, after she had endured much distress and poverty during the Commonwealth, when she was even forced to pawn "her two rings, a crosse, and a jewell of gold inlayed with rubies and diamonds." When the joy-bells of the Restoration had rung out the gloom of Puritanism, she writes from Bun-na-margie to a friend in Dublin, asking him to use his influence "to gett my old dwellynge, Ballycastle, to mee again." Whether the Countess, who was then 80 years of age, was at this time living inside the walls of the ruined Monastery, or only sheltering in some temporary refuge within its precincts to be near her dead lord, cannot now be decided with accuracy.

The present remains of the Monastery—and they clearly indicate all the main buildings that doubtless ever existed—consist of a large church 99 feet long by 24 feet 6 inches wide, showing no appearance

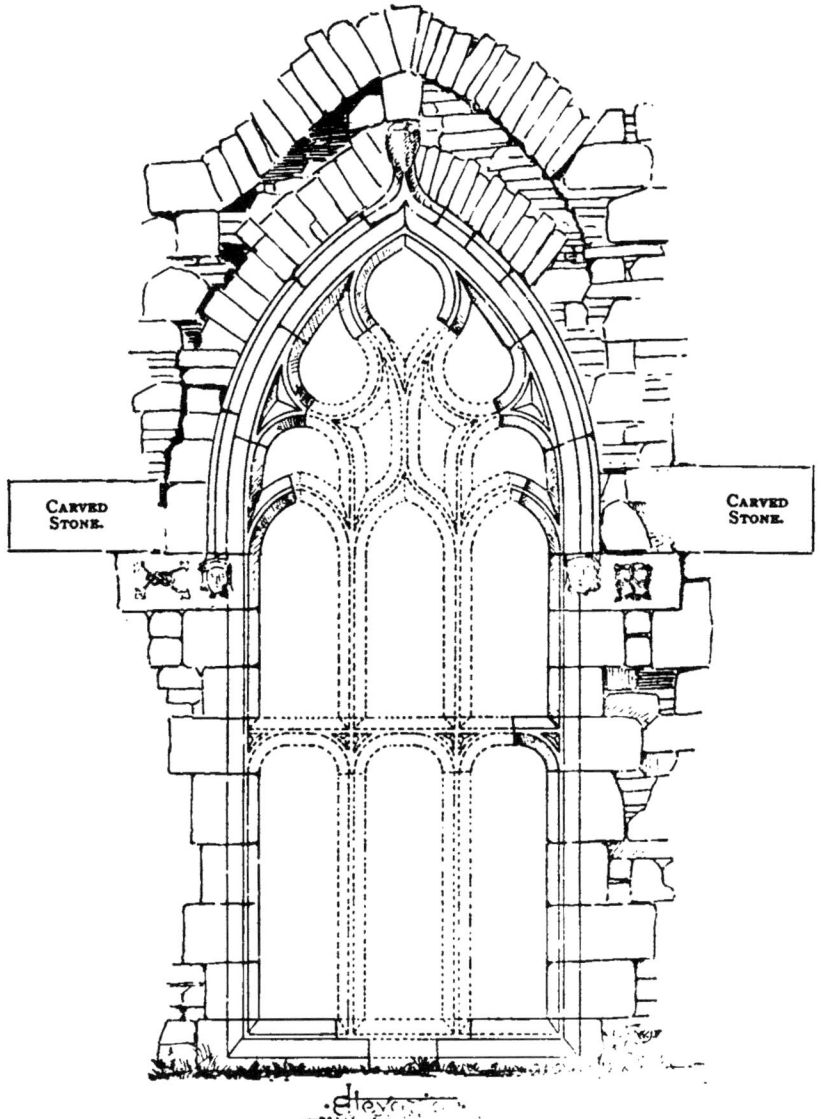

THE EAST WINDOW, SHOWING MISSING PARTS RESTORED IN DOTTED LINES.
(Scale shown on Plan.)

of division into choir and nave, and void of aisles or side chapels, being a plain rectangular structure, with the great window at the east end and three smaller ones on the south side and none on the north.

It is accurately orientated and built of Ballycastle sandstone, roughly hammered, and filled in with small field or river stones. The disappearance of the west wall has removed the door, which is traditionally supposed to have existed there, and is always referred to as one of great beauty and symmetry. Where it stood, the rude cross

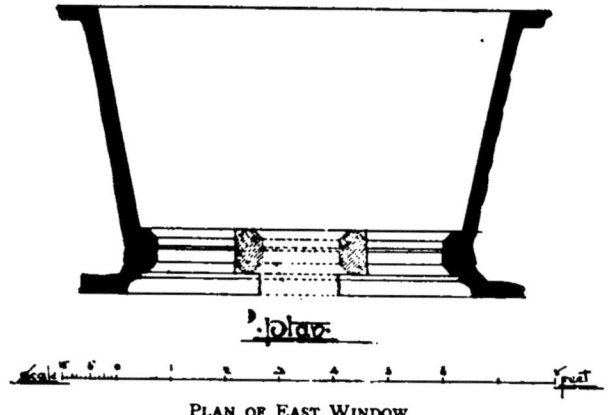

PLAN OF EAST WINDOW.

East window. over the grave of Julia MacQuillin now stands. The present east window has the look of having been inserted at a later date than the building of the church, as evidenced by the arch and appearances of insertion on the outside. The older arch is a large one, and bears a resemblance to the east window at Ardtole, near Ardglass, Co. Down.

CARVED STONE ON SOUTH SIDE OF EAST WINDOW.

From the remaining fragments of the mullions it is capable of restoration, which has been carefully done on the sketch, p. 21. It was a two-storied flamboyant window of most graceful form and beautiful proportions, and well entitled it to the designation, "The pride of the North." A most remarkable feature of the window is the interlaced carvings on either side of the terminals of the mouldings on the outside. Similar carvings are to be seen at the east window of the old church of Magheratemple on an adjoining eminence. This window is also two-storied, of a similar design to Bun-na-margie, and very beautiful.

The carving on the south side of the window represents a female head with cap and hanging lappets, whilst the ornament is cross-shaped with a central interlaced knot, the terminals expanding into

CARVED STONE ON NORTH SIDE OF EAST WINDOW.

leaves. That on the north side represents a male head also capped, the ornament being an interlaced square having a cross centre. On the course above these carved stones, but adjoining, are two other stones beautifully carved in a similar style. These stones have the appearance of having been removed from an earlier structure and built where

RAISED CARVING ON STONE BUILT INTO THE OUTSIDE OF EAST WALL, SOUTH OF EAST WINDOW.

they now are for preservation; and this is borne out by the fact that the ornament does not now show as it would have been placed originally, but transversely; and both the stones are mutilated, although quite filling their present spaces.

The stone on the south side has a long interlaced plant pattern, with square leaves at the sides, terminated by a nondescript animal with a swinging tail; whilst that to the north has a somewhat similar design, terminating in an equally indescribable animal, varied, however, by an interlaced tail. The arch-stone of the moulding is

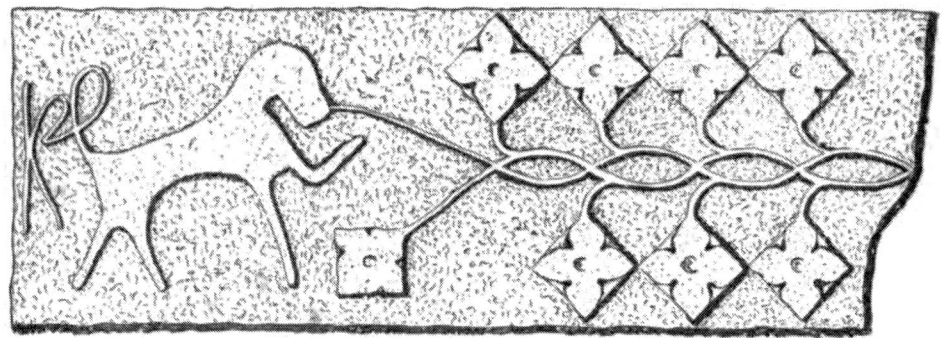

RAISED CARVING, NORTH SIDE OF EAST WINDOW.

surmounted by what may have been a head, or perhaps a cusped finial, now, however, obliterated by the storms of ages.

The altar. After the Monastery had been deserted by its occupants and the sacred vessels taken away, tradition records that they were hidden in the sandhills at a spot that would be illuminated by the light from the east window. The side stones of the altar still remain *in situ*, the one on the Gospel side having an aperture cut in it 12 in. by 18 in., but the covering stone has gone. Some say it was re-cut, and now rests in the north-east corner above the remains of "Francis Stewart, Bishop of Down and Connor," who was a Franciscan, and held the See from 1740 until 1750. There is a small door to the west end of the south wall which has the curious feature of being circular-headed inside and pointed outside. There is a beautifully carved drip-stone worked in the solid on the springer

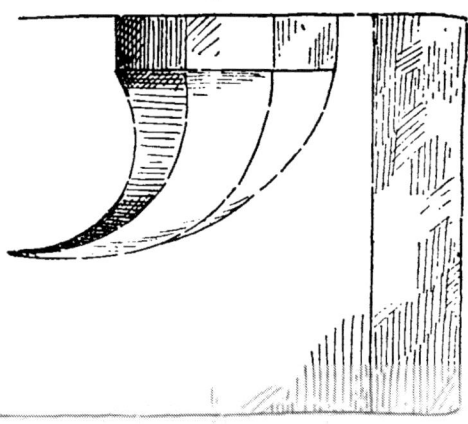

Drip-stone under hood of South Door

THE FRIARY OF BUN-NA-MARGIE.

of this door; the lable or hood which rested on it has, however, disappeared.

Two of the windows on the south are still perfect, showing flat-pointed arches outside and flat rough-built arches inside; the third window is now exposed by the destruction of a portion of the Macnaghten monument. These windows are narrow, and would not admit much light, but are good examples of 15th century work. On the south side, running at right angles to the choir and in a line with the east wall, the present Antrim vault has been erected; and as its construction is modern, bearing a slated roof, its appearance rather spoils the otherwise picturesque aspect of the ruins. Whether this vault occupies the site of an ancient transept or side chapel cannot be determined from present appearance, although there are some features to favour the supposition. Of these the built-up archway to the west of the entrance to the vault is one, the stones of which certainly have no appearance of modern cutting, but whether they have been removed from some other part of the building and inserted here, as some say, with no conceivable object however, cannot with certainty be determined. In my opinion it has been altered, but occupies its original site, and was the entrance to an earlier MacDonnell chapel or vault that existed before the present structure, which is described as having been newly roofed in the year 1833.

South windows.

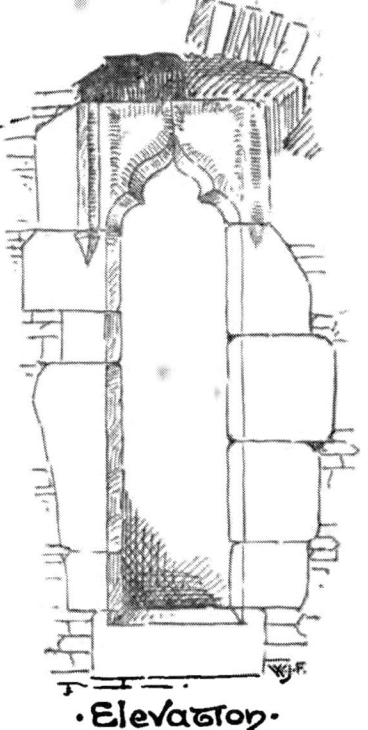
·Elevation·
WINDOW IN SOUTH WALL OF CHURCH.
(*See Plan.*)

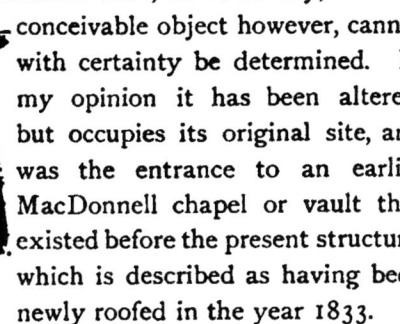
Plan
WINDOW IN SOUTH WALL OF CHURCH.

West door.

The vault and its contents will be described later on, but in dealing with the church the present door into the modern chapel above the MacDonnell vault must be mentioned. There can be no doubt that

26 THE FRIARY OF BUN-NA-MARGIE.

this door was built into its present position when the vault was erected, no matter what may be said of the adjoining arch; but, strange to say,

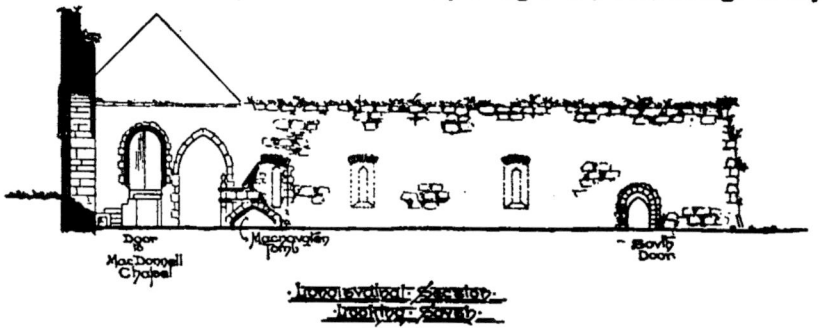

BUN-NA-MARGIE—SOUTH SECTION—INTERIOR VIEW, SHOWING DOOR INTO MACDONNELL CHAPEL, BUILT-UP ARCH, MACNAGHTEN TOMB, SOUTH WINDOWS, AND DOOR.

it has also the appearance of age, and must have come from another quarter. Can it be the west door above referred to? In my opinion the chances are that it is, yet it would not bear out the tradition of great beauty, although comely and in good taste. What is much better evidence, however, is the entire absence of the door from the west end, not even a carved stone of it remaining to be seen; whilst here

THE MONUMENT OF JOHN MACNAGHTEN, SOUTH WALL OF CHURCH.

is a well-preserved door, quite in keeping with the architecture to be expected, and quite in harmony with the interior arch of the remaining door on the south side. To use the ancient door of a MacDonnell church as a modern door to the family vault would be quite in keeping with the spirit of the times in which the vault was erected.

To the west of the built-up archway on the south wall the Macnaghten monument was erected, and to prepare a place for it a window was built up. This altar tomb, made of sandstone, was a fine one of its class, but is now, like the building around, half ruined. Why it has not been conserved by the Macnaghten family is inexplicable, seeing they are wealthy and still well represented in the district. A frieze rests upon a rather flat arch, which was supported by pilasters, surmounted by moulded terminals. From the centre of the frieze a gablette appears to have risen, but this is now almost entirely destroyed. Along the frieze the following inscription appeared, the portions missing being added in :— *Macnaghten tomb.*

HEIRE · LYETH · THE · BODIE · OF · IHN · MNAGHTEN · FIR[ST · SECRETAIRE · TO · THE]
FIRST · ERLE · OF · ANTRIM · WH · ODEP · ARTED · THIS · M[ORTAL · LIFE · IN · THE · YEAR]
OF · OVR LORD GOD
1 · 6 · 3 · 0

On the pilaster to the left-hand side, in a line with the inscription, a crosslette fitchee has been cut; this is evidently taken from the MacDonnell arms, for this John Macnaghten, or John dhu, was a nephew of the great Sorley Boy, as well as secretary to the first earl, and so was interred close to the MacDonnell vault. There are other gravestones within the church, but they are modern, and do not come within the scope of this notice.

On a line with the east wall of the church, on the north side, are the domestic buildings, consisting of a refectory 35 ft. long by 17 ft. 4 in. wide, with a smaller chamber 18 ft. 3 in. by 10 ft. 9 in., doubtless used for general purposes. This latter chamber is connected with the refectory by two square openings, not doors, but similar to serving windows, and may have been used as such; it has also two cupboards, one in the west and one in the east wall, and a door into the passage on the south side which divides it from the church. There is also a built-up doorway on the east side, which I believe was made in recent years in order to facilitate burials in this vault, *Domestic buildings. Refectory.*

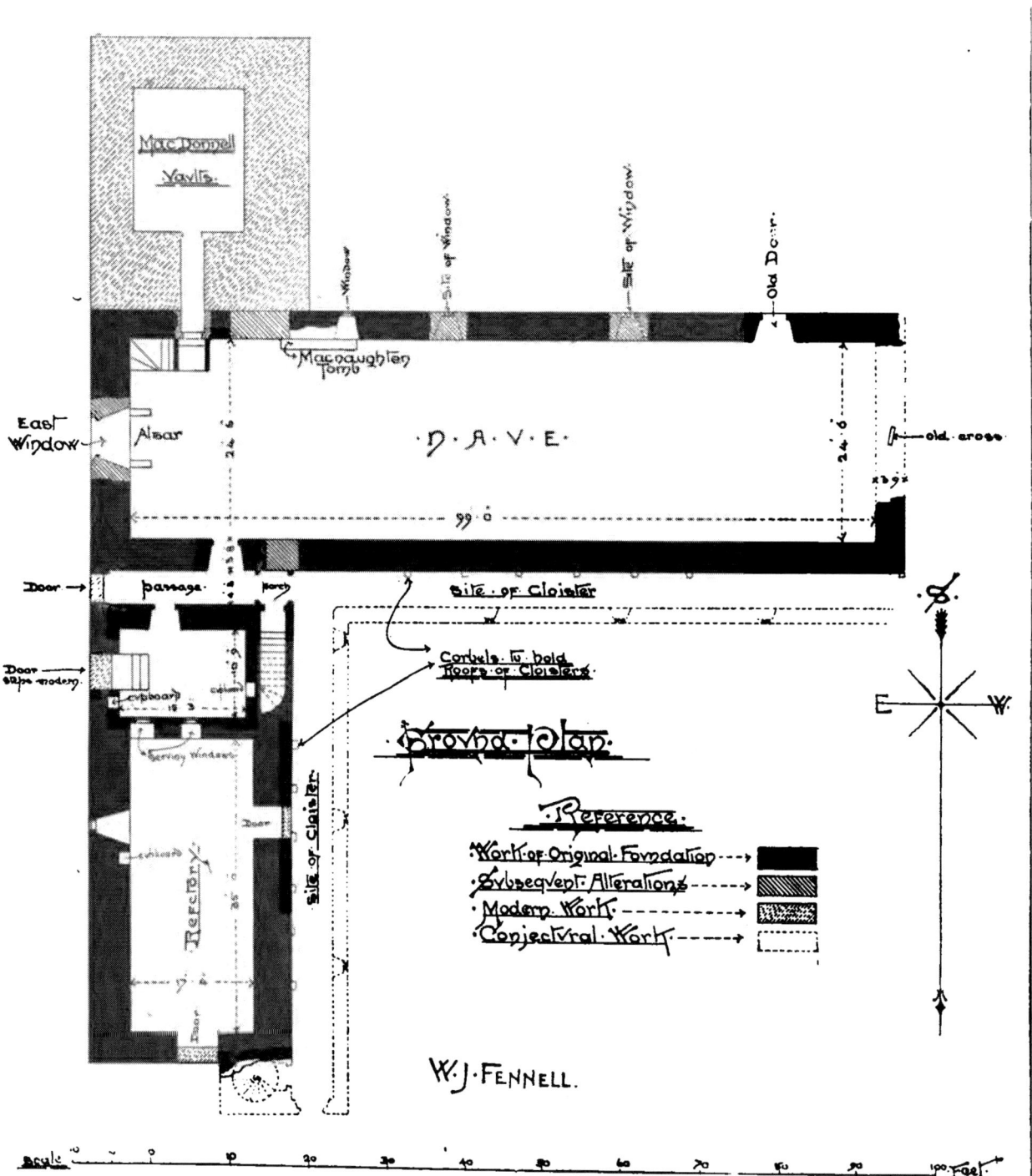

GROUND PLAN OF BUN-NA-MARGIE, SHOWING DETAILS OF BUILDINGS REFERRED TO IN TEXT.

probably replacing a window. The south door and the cupboards make it probable that this apartment was used for domestic purposes, especially as the door into the passage would lead direct to the lodge to the east of the Abbey, which served the double purpose of guest-house and kitchen, there being no fireplaces either in the refectory or smaller chamber. This door into the passage, now half built up, is very finely moulded with cut stone, displaying three distinct arches—two semicircular and one pointed. The refectory has a door in the west wall leading to the cloisters, and one in the north gable, both now built up. There is only one window, which is in the east wall, so there must have been very little light unless when the doors were open. The window is now closed on the outside where the burials have raised the earth several feet above the original level; but seen from the inside, it is one of the most perfect and beautiful features remaining. It is deeply splayed to the inside, the splay being carried round the head, all worked with great accuracy in cut stone.

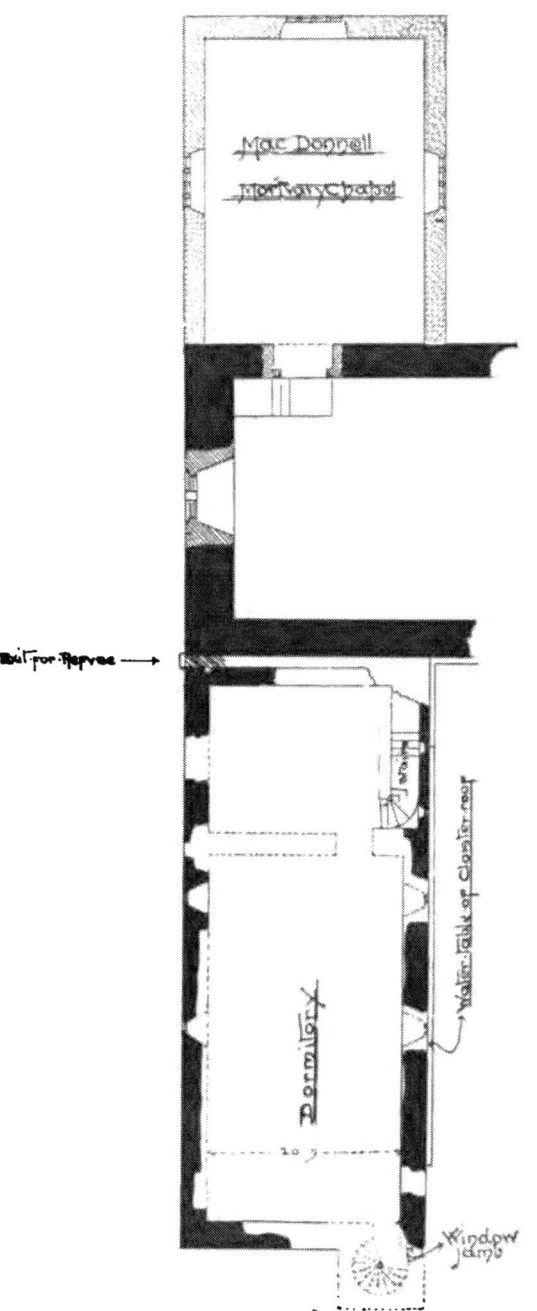

PLAN OF UPPER FLOOR OF BUN-NA-MARGIE.

30   THE FRIARY OF BUN-NA-MARGIE.

Passage adjoining Church.

The dividing passage or slype between the chamber and the church had a porch on the west side leading to the cloisters, and from this porch to the north a flight of steps in the thickness of the wall leads to the dormitories. There was also a door on the south side of this passage leading into the church, which is very beautifully arched and moulded, and the door on the east side which led to the lodge. The ground floor of the domestic buildings had heavy stone-vaulted roofs, that of the refectory running north and south, whilst that of the smaller chamber and the passage ran east and west. On the north-west corner of the refectory the remains of a small square tower can still be seen, containing a circular stair from the cloisters to the dormitories ; the latter may have been divided, thus allowing these stairs to accommodate the larger room, whilst the stairs descending to the passage adjoining the church gave access to the smaller apartment, which may have been for the Guardian, the other being for the monks. The walls of the dormitories are now only a few feet high, but two small windows are still perfect on the east wall, with traces of a third, and portion of one to light the upper part of the circular stairs. The remains of three windows can be traced in the west wall, and the two small ones still exist, which gave light to the stairs ascending from the passage. In a sketch made by A. Nicholl in 1833 the north dormitory gable is shown standing, with a large window in the centre. Between the south wall of the dormitories and the north wall of the church on the eastern side a refuse aperture was constructed. No appearance of fireplaces can be traced in this building, either above or on the ground floor. The walls of the dormitories are considerably thinner than those below, which can be accounted for by the roof being a light one, probably thatched with straw or heather, whilst the refectory is stone-vaulted. The present vaulting is covered with an accumulation of vegetable mould and fallen

Vaulting.

·Cupboard·

IN DOMESTIC DEPARTMENT.

masonry, which the rain soaks through, permeating the vaulting to the floor. This must soon, in the natural course of things, cause its collapse. As one foresees the end approaching, and remembers

Door from Domestic Apartment into Passage on North Side of Church, partly built up.

that this is the only building left in the County Antrim from which some tangible outline of monastic habitations can be formed, the thought arises that its preservation could be accomplished by the same inexpensive means as those adopted by the Board of Works at Mellifont, where, although the walls were only a few feet above the ground, they are preserved from further injury or decay by a covering of asphalt. The noble owner of this building, which was so long benefited by his ancestors, and within whose walls many of them are buried, might use his influence to have it conserved under the Board of Works, and thus ensure its preservation for future ages.

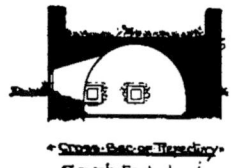

Cross-Sec. of Refectory. South End showing Serving doors.
VAULTING OF REFECTORY.

The door leading from the passage into the church through the north wall is preserved, although it now appears very low on account of the floor of the church being raised by burials and *débris*. It is 4 ft. wide and about the same in height. The ground chambers of the domestic apartments were used as burial vaults for many years, as quantities of bones were formerly visible, and tradition states that many of the MacDonnells were here interred. Within the memory of those still living, a great breach in the east wall long existed, which gave an easy access not only to visitors but to the sheep that grazed around. This has now been closed and the bones buried, the only entrance being the one from the church. To see the interior features a light is necessary, all the windows and doors being filled in. The cloisters stood at the angle formed by the north wall of the church

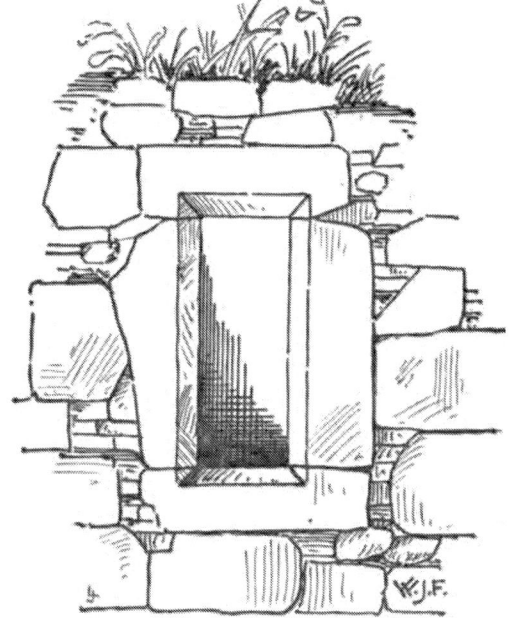

Dormitory Window.

The cloisters.

and the west wall of the domestic buildings. No traces of them at present exist except a few corbel stones and the marks of the line of roof along the walls; they were constructed of material not so strong as the remaining buildings, wood probably being used in the pillars and roof. The placing of the cloisters on the north side of the church, in such an exposed place as Ballycastle, proves that the monks courted austerities; although a cynical age may deem that the north side was protected by cloisters, whilst the sunny south wall did not require such; and if *dolce far niente* was to be enjoyed, the lee side would doubtless be taken advantage of.

Against the south wall of the church stands, transept-wise, the strongly-built slated chapel and vault of the Antrim family, as already mentioned. The upper portion is a chapel, now dismantled, the lower part is arranged for the dead, with a stone-vaulted roof. The chapel has no inside features of interest, being quite modern, with an open timber roof and three square Tudor windows, one in each side. Both chapel and vault are entered from the church by different doors, the former by a short flight of steps affixed to the south wall adjoining the altar, whilst the latter has a heavy iron door underneath the steps to the chapel.

The MacDonnell vault.

On the outside south wall of the MacDonnell vault is inserted a square stone with the following raised inscription :—

Mural Tablet in the South Gable of the Mac Donnell Chapel.

The first three lines of the inscription and part of the fourth, with the date, are well-nigh weathered out of recognition, and can only with great difficulty be traced. The re-cutting of this stone by the Earl of Antrim is a pressing necessity, if the inscription is to be made legible. The preservation of this stone in its present position leads to the conclusion that this was not the first MacDonnell vault, but only takes the place of a former one which may have stood on the same site. The date 1621, with that on the Macnaghten tomb, 1630, also go to prove that the whole church had undergone some renovation at this time to suit the requirements of the MacDonnell clan, after the destruction heaped upon the buildings by the fire of 1584, when Sorley Boy burned the English out of their encampment within its walls.

Sheltering priests.

The very year of the erection of this stone by the *Comes de Antrim*, saw his Lordship summoned to Dublin by the Lord Deputy, Grandison, on a charge of having sheltered priests in his castle, as before mentioned. After some courtly talk—which meant in plain English that Lord Antrim could do pretty much as he liked in religious matters—eschewing any interference from the English Crown, he continued so to act for many years, until clouds of more portent began to gather around the head of the martyr king. For over thirty years Lord Antrim afforded ample hospitality in his houses at Dunluce, Dunanannie, and Glenarm to a proscribed priesthood; and it is not a big stretch of imagination, when we know that he did so, to also conclude that the fabric of the family shrine at Bun-na-margie received some attention, and at least the church may have been restored to its former uses and condition. Many things go to prove the Earl to have been ardent in his religion. He had a son, Francis—not by his wife, the daughter of the Earl of Tyrone—who had donned the Franciscan habit, and would doubtless have been Guardian of Bun-na-margie had not the times changed. The northern bishops unsuccessfully petitioned the Pope that he should be appointed to the See of Clogher; one of the arguments considered of great moment and used in his favour was that "he, owing to his sire's connections with many of the principal families of England and Scotland, will be comparatively free in the exercise of his sacred calling."

Saint Brigid's Wells.

It is also recorded that the Earl visited with his wife, she being childless, the celebrated wells of Saint Brigid in the County of Roscommon, and afterwards, their prayers being answered, enclosed the same with a wall, into which a stone was inserted bearing the

MacDonnell arms and the inscription—"Built by the Right Honourable Randall McDonnell, first Earl of Antrim, 1625."

It is thus evident that the powerful protection of the Earl was willingly extended to the Church and the clergy, until he was laid at rest in old Bun-na-margie in the year 1636.

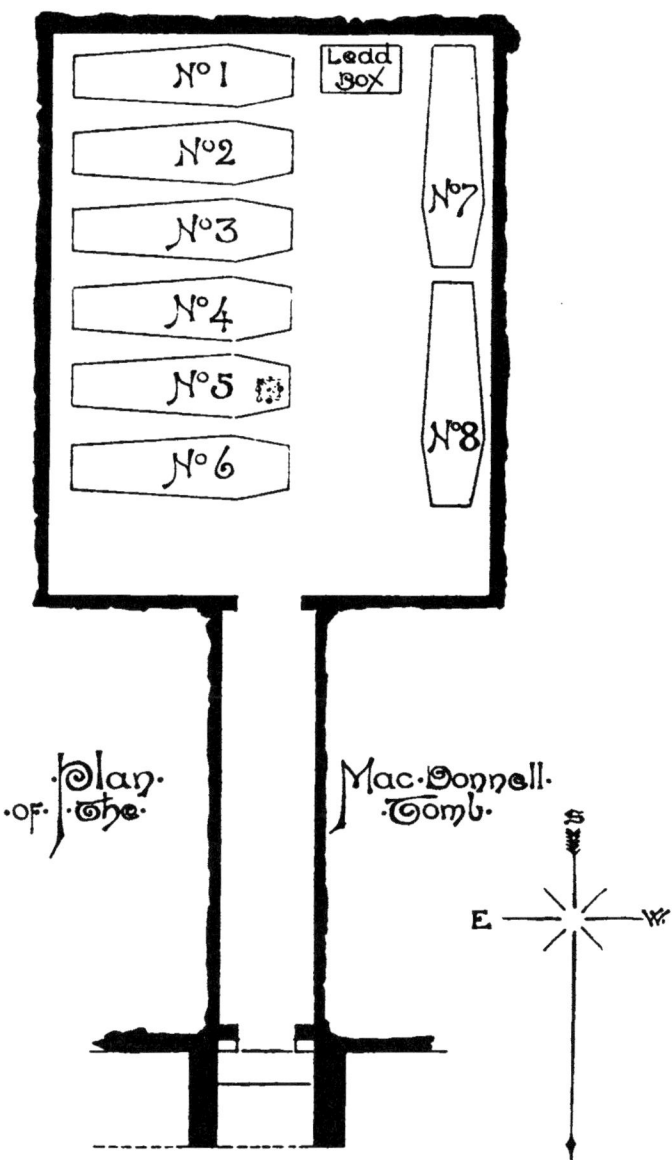

The vault contains eight coffins and a small lead box, which will be described in detail.

The MacDonnell coffins.

No. 1.—Lead coffin with brass plate, bearing the following three inscriptions in Gaelic, Saxon, and Latin:—

> Mór an beud bár uí Cholla
> Do Leath-Cuinn 'r don taobh-tuaith
> Cearnaidh go deirgh rilear orra
> O ló pagno rill cum an uaig.

The Most Hon[bl] RANDLE, Lord Marquis of
    Antrim.
Borne the 9th day of June, in yeare
of God, 1610; died y[e] 3rd day of Feb., 1682.

> *Invictus patriæ Caroli Randelle Deique*
> *Hoc plumbo resides aureus ipse pugil*
> *Cujus inadversa Bellonæ sorte rebelles*
> *Hedere vel furcæ non potuere fidem.*

No. 2.—Oak coffin and brass plate.

The Most Noble RANDLE WILLIAM M[c]DONNELL,
Marquis of Antrim, Earle of Antrim, Viscount Dunluce
of the Glens, and Baron of Antrim,
Govenor of the County of Antrim,
Knight of the Most Noble and Militry Order of the Bath,
and one of His Majesty's Most Hon. Privy Council.

His Lordship was born 4th Nov., 1719, and departed this
    Life 28 July, 1791.

No. 3.—Oak coffin covering a lead coffin.

The Right Honourab[le]
ALEXANDER M[c]DONNELL,
Earl of Antrim.
Aged 62.
Died 1st October. M. the 13th, 1775.

No. 4.—Oak coffin.

ANN, Countess
of Antrim.
Died
14th Jan[ry], 1753.
Aged 37 years.

THE FRIARY OF BUN-NA-MARGIE.

No. 5.—Velvet-covered coffin, brass mounted, with arms and full-sized coronet on cushion.

HUGH SEYMOUR M^cDONNELL,
7th Earl of Antrim
and
Viscount Dunluce,
Son of
Vice-Admiral Lord Mark Robert Kerr,
Son of William, 5th Marquis of Lothain,
and of
Charlotte,
In her own right
2nd Countess of Antrim and
Viscountess Dunluce,
3rd daughter of Randall William,
6th Earl and 2nd Marquis of Antrim.
Born 7th August, A.D. 1812.
Died 18th of July, A.D. 1855,
In the 43rd year of his age.

No. 6.—Velvet-covered coffin with coronet.

LAURA CECILIA,
Widow of
Hugh Seymour McDonnell,
7th Earl of Antrim.
Born 30th May,
1808.
Died 26th Jan^{ry},
1883.

Nos. 7 and 8.

These are the two oldest coffins, and are much decayed, the lids having fallen in and the remains being exposed. Both contain skeletons of full-grown persons, one of whom may have been Sir Randal, first Earl of Antrim, and the other the last Lord Slane, the great-grandson of the first Earl of Antrim, who fought at the Boyne and retired to France with James, his vast estates being forfeited. He fled from Dublin to escape the smallpox, and was thrown from his horse near Ballycastle and seriously injured. When he recovered consciousness, he found himself in a fever-stricken cottage, with his head in the poor woman's lap. He caught the infection, and succumbed to the disease he had fled from Dublin to avoid. He died in 1728, and is stated to have been buried in this vault. The small square sealed lead box at the south end is believed to contain the remains of Sorley Boy, gathered together on their removal into the present vault. All the coffins, save Nos. 7 and 8, are laid facing the east, and the vault and its stone benches are in excellent order.

<small>Lord Slane.</small>

The Irish inscription on the first coffin may be translated thus—

Great the loss, the death of the descendant of Colla,
To Conn's Half and to the North
This last affliction befell them
Since the day Randall turned to the grave.

The Latin on same coffin thus—

> O Randal, unconquered friend of Country, of Charles, and of God, thou now liest in this lead thyself a golden warrior, whose fidelity in the adverse lot of battles rebels nor gibbets were not able to bend.

The Ladies O'Neill. It is a curious fact that the three Ladies O'Neill were not buried with their lords in Bun-na-margie. Mary, the wife of Sorley Boy, sleeps with her own kindred at Armagh; Alice, the wife of Randal, the first Earl of Antrim, lies in her native Tyrone; whilst Rose, the wife of Randal the Magnificent, the first Marquis of Antrim, was buried beside her father and mother in the Church of St. Nicholas at Carrickfergus.

And so repose the mighty, the great, the turbulent; a few weak planks or a little lead hold those whom armies failed to conquer, stratagem to encompass, or treachery to drag down.

> "Have them in Thy holy keeping!
> God, be with them lying sleeping!"
> *Sir S. Ferguson.*

Documents found in vault. In the year 1820 an oak chest was opened in the Antrim vault, and in it several documents were found. One of them consisted of a portion of a manuscript copy of the works of Thomas Aquinas, done on parchment in mediæval Latin, extending to about 600 pages. The date was the fourteenth century, and it was originally brought from the Monastery of Saint Anthony of Amiens in France, of which Francis MacDonnell, before mentioned, was for some time Guardian. Another manuscript was a fifteenth century translation of Saint Bonaventure's *Life of Christ*, consisting of 35 two-column pages, with initials beautifully illuminated in gold and surrounded by flowers of various hues, in good preservation. At the beginning of the present century a rod of gold was found in the adjoining stream. It was 38 inches long, and terminated in hooks at both ends. The rod was over 20 oz. in weight, and was made of three wires twisted together. This valuable relic is not now known to exist; so, like many other similar finds, it has probably passed into the jeweller's melting-pot. In 1851 a wrought gilt key was found near the ruins, and was, I believe, deposited in the Royal Irish Academy, but after faithful search I have failed to discover it. A few years later a storm disclosed, amongst the sand close to the ruins, some fragments of crosses and book covers, and a small round silver box, which was subsequently made into a pyxis for use in Ballycastle Chapel.

THE FRIARY OF BUN-NA-MARGIE. 39

At a distance of 21 yards from the Friary, in an easterly direction, Gate lodge. stands the most distinctly picturesque portion of the ruins, isolated and alone, yet associated with the main buildings. The little guest-

THE GATE LODGE, GUEST-HOUSE, OR KITCHEN.

house, gate lodge, or kitchen, or all three combined, is unique in its way. It is about 19 ft. 3 in. long by 13 ft. 3 in. wide, and is built north and south, two stories high, the northern gable showing a high tottering chimney of cut stone. Both the east and west walls of this chamber show large gateways, thus forming a passage through, although not directly opposite to each other; whilst the upper chamber had a large chimney in the north gable and a small

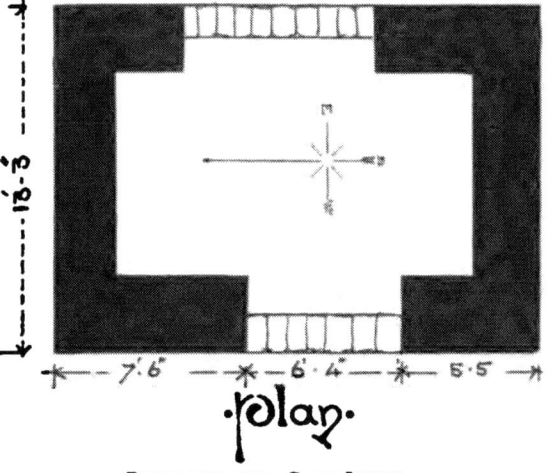

BUN-NA-MARGIE—GATE LODGE.

square window in the south gable. No vestige of the floor now exists, so it must have been of wood; nor are there any remains of an ascending stair. The existence of the fireplace, the only one to be seen in all the buildings, goes far to prove that this upper room was used as a kitchen, whilst the large doors on both sides of the ground floor affirm conclusively that a through passage or gateway was intended. It may be that the grounds immediately surrounding the Monastery were fenced in, either with a mound or a stockade, of which no portion now exists, and that lawful entrance was alone effected through this lych gate, where a member of the community would always remain; or it may be that this was a hospital or guest-house, and that the extra luxury of a fire denied to the community was given to patients or guests. The whole building has the appearance and similarity of style of the domestic buildings of the Monastery.

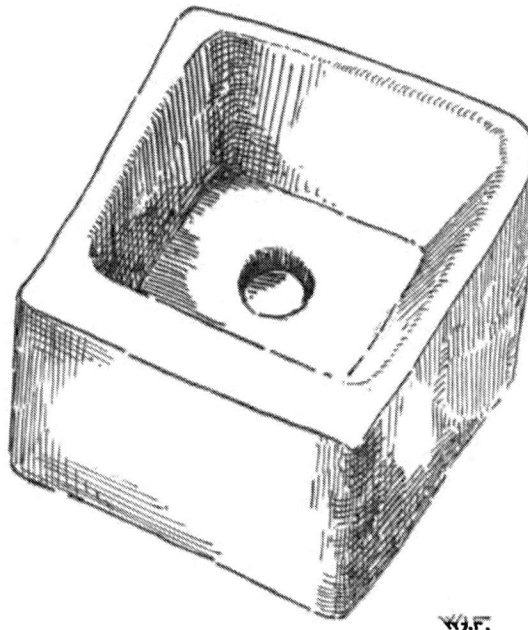
HOLLOWED STONE IN CHURCHYARD.

Hollowed Stones.

In the churchyard, a little to the east of the Antrim vault, are two stones with large square holes cut in them. These appear to be too rude for fonts, although they may have been such, but it is more likely they were sockets for crosses or other erections.

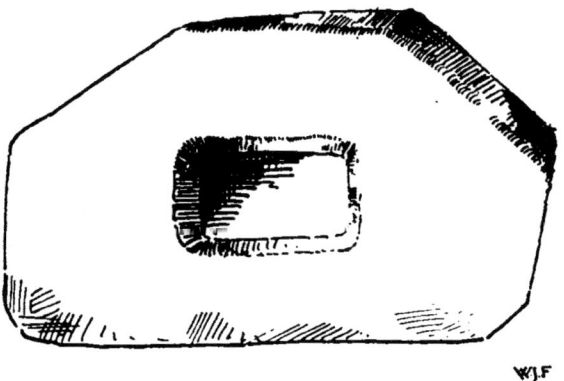
HOLLOWED STONE IN CHURCHYARD.

There are only three stones in the graveyard having heraldic bear-

THE FRIARY OF BUN-NA-MARGIE.

ings upon them. They bear the names of MacDonnell, MacKay, and Ker, families long connected with the district, and all of Scottish origin. The first or MacDonnell stone is close to the south wall of the church, and bears the full family arms with supporters cut on the east side, the date being 1764. The MacKay stone is dated 1736, and bears the arms boldly cut on the west, the inscription being on the east side. The Ker stone is dated 1738, and has the shield cut on the east side with a portion of the inscription, the remainder being on the west side.

ALEXANDER MCDONNELL WROUGHT THIS MONUMENT FOR HIS FAMILY HERE LY- ETH HIS DAUGHTER FRANCES MCDONNELL WHO DIED MAY THE 13TH 1763 AGED 3 QUARTERS
   MEMENTO MORI

The inscription on the following stone is on the east face, whilst the arms are cut on the back. The stone is 3 in. thick, 24 in. broad, and 25 in. high, and lies, like the Ker stone, east of the church.

HERE LYETH YE
BODY OF DANIEL
MCKAY WHO DIED
APRIL YE 2D 1736 AGED
30 YEARS

The following stone of the Ker family is 5½ in. thick and 24 in. broad, sunk in the earth.

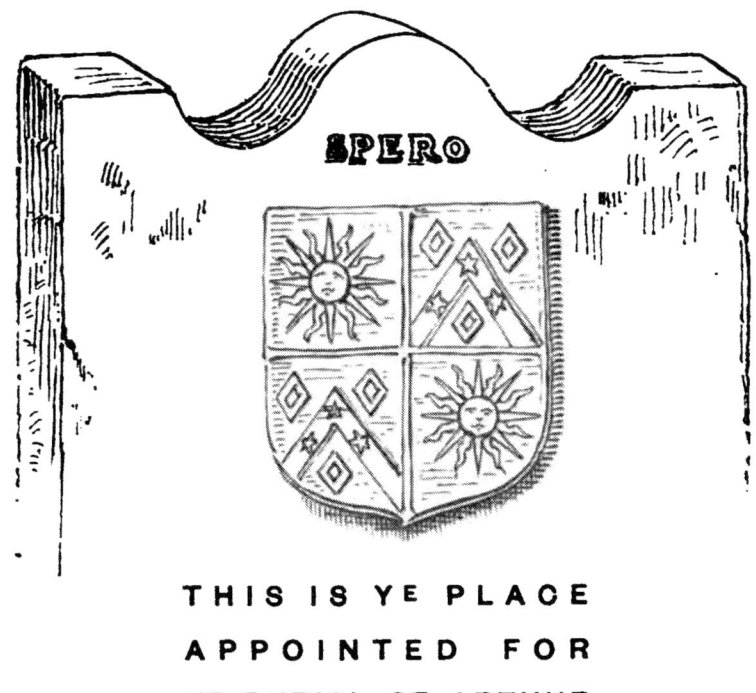

THIS IS YE PLACE
APPOINTED FOR
YE BURIAL OF ARTHUR
KER & HIS FAMILY

On the back is cut the following inscription:—

I H S

HERE LYETH YE BODY
OF ARTHUR KER WHO
DIED NOVER YE 15TH 1738
AGED 1 YEAR

There are also two other monuments—large flat slab-stones—with inscriptions worthy of recording. The first belongs to the Daragh family, and has a quaint semi-heraldic device with death emblems at the bottom of the inscription. This stone has been wrongly laid facing the west, having been carelessly transposed at the time of some burial. The stone is 6 ft. 3½ in. long, 8 in. deep, and 2 ft. 6 in. wide. The following is a copy of the inscription :—

> HERE LYETH THE BODY
> OF JOHN DARAGH WHO DIED
> AUGUST Y 15TH 1745 AGED 1
> YEAR ALSO ESTHER DAR-
> AGH DIED MAY YE 22D 1744
> AGED 2 YEARS CHILDREN
> TO ARCHBALD DARAGH
> ALSO THE SD ARCHBALD
> DIED APRIL THE 11TH
> 1762 AGED 45 YEARS

The MacMichael monument is also a flat table tomb, the inscription being almost obliterated, and only transcribed after considerable difficulty. It is 6 ft. 4 in. long, 2 ft. 11 in. wide, and 7 in. thick. A cherub, all head and wings, surmounts the inscription, which reads as follows :—

> HERE LYETH THE BODY OF
> MARY MCMICHAEL WHO DIED
> AUGUST THE 4TH 1714 AGED [ ]
> NEALE MCMICHAEL DIED MARCH
> THE 16TH 1757 ALSO JOHN MC
> MICHAEL DIED MARCH THE
> 15 1753 AND MARY MCMICHA-
> EL DIED OCTOBER THE 27
> 1755 CHILDREN TO IDOUGAL
> MCMICHAEL OF EKERVELEY
> WHOSE AGE WAS 54 YEARS

It will be noted how very young some of the persons above recorded died, and it will also be observed how Scotch the names are. This is, however, very common in the Antrim glens, where all the peasantry bear such names, clearly denoting them followers of the Clan MacDonnell, lords of the Isles and the Glynns.

I have not given in the text many details of the different measurements, relying on the very accurate and beautiful plans and measured details made for this book by William J. Fennell, architect, Belfast.

THE FRIARY OF BUN-NA-MARGIE. 45

My task is finished. I have recorded in a brief, broken, and discon- Conclusion.
nected manner all I know, what I have observed, what is recorded in
books, and many things kind friends have told me, concerning the
dismantled, storm-battered ruins of the one time famous Franciscan
Monastery of Bun-na-margie, around whose walls have raged
the fights of centuries, the clang of swords, the burning shot, the
exultant cry of the victors, and the deep groans of the wounded and
the dying, and within whose precincts repose the men of peace side
by side with those who revelled in war and in the rumours of war,
to whom the red flag of carnage was a sight to gladden the eye and
thrill the blood, quickening the arm to further deeds of rapine and
slaughter. Now all is peace, the sun shines and the dew of heaven
falls equally on the just and the unjust, and the mortal remains of
each have returned to their common mother, the earth, from whence
they were created, whilst their spirits have departed to that Otherland,
happy or otherwise, each to reap the reward of the deeds done in the
flesh.

THE TOMB OF THE EARLS. *(From a Photo.)*

Printed by Libri Plureos GmbH in Hamburg, Germany